GRAVITY'S PLUMB LINE

ROSS LECKIE

GASPEREAU PRESS
PRINTERS & PUBLISHERS
Kentville, Nova Scotia
2005

For Kathryn Taglia

CONTENTS

I

The Saint John River

LITTLE ST. JOHN LAKE

The frowzy lake covered with weed
is merely a little spilled water,
afterthought to an afternoon's rain.

It is a cloudy day, the clouds touched
just once lightly in purple ink.
The mosquitoes will be out later.

French and English spill over this
splash of greeny brown and murky
green. Or they would if anyone

were here—they do back in St. Aurelie
where the leak of water trickling north
briefly marks a border between

Québec and Maine. But this is the
place where it all begins, the lake
a crystal pitcher tipping its liquid

into a trick of evening light.
Brackish, shallow, a seep through
the furze and spindly spruce, it moves

as if it has all the time in the world—
and it does; a foot sinks in the soft mud,
icy water slips over the lip of your boot.

You feel that just one of these lily pads
should answer for human suffering. And
wouldn't that be the ache of their bulbous

flowers? Each pad is a large green eye
and they stare and stare and stare. Each
is an ear connected by an auditory nerve

to the brain-muck of the lake's bottom.
Lily pads are the horizontal and the sedge
nearby is the vertical. The pads are set

to register every ripple of the water's
moody funk. The grasses quiver, listening
to the slightest whisper of the heated air.

Like the missing sequence in a strand
of DNA or a genealogy that vanishes
into the unknown of your great grandfather,

the First St. John Pond has evaporated.
Second, Third, Fourth and Fifth ponds
flow down to the blue stipple of Baker Lake.

The lily pads shadow and blacken the water,
so the fish can slip by unnoticed, dreamlike,
fantastical, each a distinct theology.

ALLAGASH

The stones are so utterly nameless.
They don't think. Each is an obdurate
anti-philosophy, each the insistent

stony refusal in the cobbled water's
brittle fluidity. The water moves its
quiet weight in bewilderment, presses

its clammy hands around these hardened things
and tries to soften them in its slow grinding.
Each stone is a death in the family,

caught in the throat of the river,
each like a tombstone marked
by the striations of sunlight bent by

the current's impurities, marbled
across the river's bottom. How
could we not admit that the river

in such a place, in its ginger transparency,
is the open mouth of joy? We make
the mistake of thinking only of song,

that rocks sing or are silent. We don't
notice the incessant splash, the noise of it,
the rocks batting at the sunlight's sparkle

with their flickering paws. We don't consider
the ecstatic hush, this gesture of healing,
its nameless naming over and over again.

EDMUNDSTON

It carries the burden of human effluent,
and we are amazed at how transparently
it is absorbed. At sunset a watercolour sky

leaves magenta in the wisps of cirrus
and livid pink in the sky behind the town.
Indigo is in the low ruffle of cloud,

and an orange the acidic shade of rind
is burnt into the horizon. This wash
seeps into the river's nocturnal reflections,

where it deepens into sombre shades
of burgundy and charcoal. The river
coming out of the bush could have had no

knowledge of this conflagration of human
dispersal. The pulp and paper chimney
raising its black finger up from the skyline

shoots its perpetual anger into the sky,
but the sky cools and gentles it, slows
the plume into a gorgeous mauve that

puffs and billows into quiet evaporation.
Beneath the water's darker ruffled reds
the chimney like a squid jets its black ink.

GRAND FALLS

The houses unweight from their foundations
and seem to float on the river, believing they
are houseboats tethered to shoreline maples.

Only the church and the mill hold back,
like old men dipping their toes to the cold,
shivering against the immersion faith requires.

Rusted sunlight perforates the leaves, but in
water's shimmer of calm deeper shades gravitate,
profound as the green of a single pine needle

unwinding its eternity on the river's surface.
The houses turn slowly over darker water
where in moonlit frosting a sister and brother

walk from parlour to hallway and up the stairs
toward the creaking floor of their parents'
bedroom, the planks of wood dry and dented,

soft and smudged to the feet the way ash feels
when rubbed between thumb and finger.
Sister, brother, and parents drift out over the falls

and hover in their sleep, watching the houses
splinter in the gorge below. The mist presses
its dampened cloth close to their fevered heads.

Pine trees lean their trunks from the cliff's edge
into sculpted air as if they were angels reaching
their feathery limbs to cradle the sleeping bodies.

I knew that I could die, but looking through
the wooden slats of the covered bridge,
an eight-year-old, a comfortable hand in

my father's, I realized he would die too.
It was pleasant to stand in the gloom,
aware of the blistering brightness at each end.

I wondered why the timbers weren't painted
like a house. We both loved the "thunka-thunka"
of the planks as a rusted pickup lumbered over them.

"The world's longest." From one end to
the other. A name can tell you everything
you want to know. A name can say that

this is a place where everything is dear.
For a moment I thought the heart carved
in the board was my father's: RL loves DB.

I looked through the boards at the tawny
colour of the water, lit by the light, so
heartlessly transparent, its hands washed clean.

BELOW FLORENCEVILLE

This is how we live here, not in the faster current
with its stark smell of going somewhere,
but in the idleness of the pool's eddy

as it circles around the place of its being.
The water is slightly brackish, the silt
on the bottom releasing its occasional

bubble of oxygen, a few individual weeds
growing toward the muted glitter of the light.
The flies are like motes of dust, visible

only in an afternoon angle of sun.
They shimmer in a cloud of unknowing,
flickering like the electrical storm

of a brain seeking constantly to shape itself.
The leaves waver in the somnolent stillness,
as if they were communicants being called

by the bell of a distant church. We take our
sustenance here, a day braided into the bread
of forgetting, as if we had always known

this place would be ours, like a farm inherited
by children who have moved to the city,
have settled, who are at home there now.

WOODSTOCK

The dead must feel the weather in their bones.
Their chins chatter with the gossip of the wind
on a winter's night; they speak of wounds that

never congeal, they listen to the guitar notes
of the ice. They lie in their eternal beds, thinking
of how long it is, how late, and they picture

how incredibly blue the sky will be in the morning.
I think I know their squabble of community,
why they never want to be alone. They rest

in an ageless colloquy in the shadow of the church.
The clapboard comforts them as it comforts me—
nothing so exquisitely weathered could be malign.

They consider how to build their souls. They make
them out of durable stone and carve their names
on them. They feel the pressing of a weight.

So what is water to them and why do they
perch on a point of land that takes the very
brunt of the storm? It must be the way light

reflects from the river's hand-polished surface,
the way the water dreams of summer talk,
of being so much alive as are the dead.

MACTAQUAC DAM

From their submerged fields the milk cows
staggered dripping and shiny onto the shore.
They wandered into the grasses to ruminate

on the goodness of grass. Their eyes were
watery and sunken in brown as if they were
pebbles drawn from the fraudulent depths.

They wonder where all the houses have gone.
It was the farmer who told me: "the oldest ones
were moved to King's Landing when they flooded

the valley here up to Woodstock. Now and then
a tree breaks loose from the bottom and a man
was killed when one rocketed right into his boat."

His tractor hammers its way up the muddy tracks
of the sloping field. A surprise of wildflowers
is tangled through the bent and the yarrow.

This is our story churning through the turbine,
its crackle of wit in the electrical wires.
Beneath the dam the channels between

islands are so shallow you can hear the flat
of the boat's bottom drag like the fricatives
of a thesaurus sliding across a table.

*

Above the dam the river undulates into belly
and udder, sways in the trundle of current
where the dam is a holding pen for water.

GOVERNMENT HOUSE

The movement of the river is a parable
told over and over, its meaning a polished stone.
You hold it damp and chill in the palm

of your hand, rub along its grain
with your thumb. If the river is unending story,
then the stone is the irreducible keepsake.

But what is a stone if not the coagulate
of a morning mist obscuring the sensible?
The very stone you hold can evaporate.

Even this pile of stone needed to be restored
to its imperial lustre, the furniture dispersed
and auctioned now reacquired through

governance of a household budget,
its appointments and lavish grounds
indifferent to the Maliseet camps struck

so long ago. It is not a tongue–the stone can tell
so little of itself, but you toss it back into the water
and the rings it makes elongate with the current,

stretching anecdotes of the morning's occurrences.
As if water is a granite to be cut and quarried,
fashioned into this extravagant mansion of daylight.

The slow reassuring ease of the water
as it loops around the stone pediments
verifies the duration of a moment's measure.

The jam of logs, buckle of ice, the floods
are not biblical, but a local passage
in our book of common prayer; the mumble

of voices, liturgical, flows into turgid air
the way the undercurrents push to a swell
of surface and fold in on themselves

in a threaded twist, a skein of liquid time.
That day we walked the bridge from end to end
we stood above it, a literal transcendence,

and I thought of what it would be to jump,
to fold the body like a single autumn leaf
and flicker downward through the overlapping

whispers of the past. The starlings chittered
in the superstructure, a calling from beam
to beam, just out of reach, girders the colour

of rafters after a fire. The water raveled,
but I froze the motion by claiming one swirl
and following it as far as the eye could travel.

GAGETOWN

The river divides and wanders around
low marsh islands of grass, as if thinking
through puzzling thickets of soft muddy ground

that seemed so clear upstream. It is blinking
back the tears of a previous rain. Still,
today you long to feel your feet sinking

into a tangy muck, to have their fill
of the condensing wheeze, to hold the thought
that flows by so insistently, until

you wonder now if the lurching stick caught
in the water's drab dun and amber roil
isn't moving against the current, jot

of a slender notion, a playful coil
of surface that eddies back into time.
This is a trick of the eye, this turmoil

of silty clay suspended in a grime
of motion; as is the uncanny sense
that the river in perpetual rhyme

doubles back around the island, repents
its alluvial squander and returns
its liquid-freshened sludge in recompense.

It is merely an effect of the Bay of Fundy,
backwash from the tide, a sour taste in the mouth.
But it is the wrong sort of nostalgia that recalls

the pure source, the first time you held
a tremulous glass of water on your own,
that kind of clarity and its refreshment.

And when you look down from the cliffs
you realize the water is a mirror and you
are looking at yourself, at the swirl as it turns

through its gut-wrenching confabulations
of current like two tired boxers who drape
their arms around each other and stagger

across the ring too stupefied to throw a punch.
For this moment you ache to be someone else.
But then it is not you, of course, it is the city.

On the other shore the cars are squeezing
out of the factory gates into the flow of traffic,
winding back to the sleep they left in the morning.

And even if it isn't the way you imagined it,
it is sustainable, this life, this back and forth.
You can imagine it now in the waning light.

SAINT JOHN HARBOUR

The sound of a young boy's shout echoes
from a warehouse wall, but you turn and no
one's there. It's as if they all went to sea

and no one came back. The ships themselves
have all gone, and, relentlessly ruffled by the
wind, the sea is a permanently unmade bed.

The sheets are draped over a laundry line
and ripple, mimicking the harbour's
white caps. The city is a rocking chair,

the streets rising and falling at odds and ends,
creaking in the bones of their calcific age.
The world seems a little harder, heavier.

On the wharf the dead weight in a clutter
of newly painted buoys, slumped as if bored
in a classroom, dreaming of a life at sea.

A red helium balloon lifts over the red brick
warehouses, escaped from a birthday or
retirement. It jerks back and forth in the breezes

that map a shifting boundary of land and water.
The cranes at the dry docks remain
motionless, hovering over the harbour's

slip like parents whose children have left
home, necks stretched in a continual
surprise that they aren't still cuddled in bed.

The water continues to rise and fall, to rise,
like the cavern of the chest, to inhale a clarity
of sunlight, to exhale the water's oxygen blue.

It is so quiet when it is like this: you can hear
the industrial hum: it is like breathing, like
an old person's breathing in a converted hotel.

II

THE ICE BIRD

In the crook of the branch
a little nest of snow.
And on a puff of wind arrives
the ice bird, where it settles to brood.
It is of a brooding mind.

You can't really see the ice bird,
but if you've ever stared
at the feathers of frost on an
old storm window,
you know how a gust

can snatch one quill
and leave its feathery print
etched on the skin of your eye.
The ice bird doesn't nestle
to warm its eggs.

They crack in the cold
and open to voices that sound
like the squeak of branches
swaying to catch the snow
as it falls. Birders will tell you

that to glimpse the ice bird
you turn the dial
on your binoculars ever
so slowly in and out of focus
until you see a glimmer of light.

Once I swear I saw one in flight
zip past my face
in a dervish of snow.
I do not want to know just
what I saw. They say an ice bird

takes seconds to whittle its prey.
Bones are taken back to the nest
and polished into a clack of ice.
If you go for a walk, the cry
of the ice bird is under your feet.

SONG FOR A WINTER DAY

He was deaf. The feather of a crow
had been placed in each ear. He could look
into the grey plumage of the sky

and hear only the throat's muffled gurgle.
There was a sound that would work
its way down the cochlear whorls

of his inner ear and unwind itself
on his brain like a needle scraping
an old vinyl record. Sometimes it had

the dirge-like thickness of Beethoven
in a late string quartet, and at others
the starry mass of a Bruckner symphony.

The tree in his yard had a nest of mulch
that looked like undigested muck dredged
from a gutter after a fall run-off.

Then one day a crow appeared
on a branch, like a case of mistaken identity,
an inky thumbprint. Its squawk

was awkward and he understood
the agility of silence now cracked
open like a walnut, after his drum

had been pricked by the tip of an icicle
he had turned and turned in his head
to freeze the sobbing melt that had

curdled there. For the first time in his life
he could hear all the birdsongs: the winter
birds, the juncos and chickadees. In spring

he was astonished by robins and the sparkle
of finches. He'd thought they all had
the same song. They were all different.

PINE

One clutch of needles stitched to the palm
of a hand extends upward into a bat of snow.

The hunger of the needles. That pang.
That green the colour of absolute zero

and polished with a glowering sheen of ice.
Each needle has a temper of fine steel.

It is my arthritic hand that is nailed
to the wood. Correction: it is merely

my hand lying open but for the fingers
bent to hold the cotton as to a wound.

FOOTFALL

A spider plummets from the acoustic tile,
landing on the desk in an inaudible explosion

of dust. Lunar silt billows from the feet
of the module on its impact with the moon.

A slender thread of silk connects these two
events and catches them in the web's

cradle of concentration. Love is in the details.
In the clap of my foot in this long corridor.

The shuffle of the cattle in the field
and the bump of their swaying carcasses
argues a congenial Sunday homeliness.

They abide by each other in slow chewing,
the grunt and snuffle as they grind
shoulder to flank in familial debate.

They move the way icebergs are calved,
the intelligent dumbness of mass,
tails flicking the pestilent hum of flies.

Their heads nod in collegial agreement
that a collision of flab is a kind of comfort
from cold radiated by shrinking snow.

And it is comfort to know the ponderous
stumble over rock and mud, the stench,
the familiar belch of the adjacent beast.

Bach's "Mass in B-Minor" carries the lowing
blats of the cornets, the low wheezing
of the woods, the grumbling of the bass

melodies, the scratching across the violins,
the clambering of voices in the "Credo"
climbing through scales and impossible

harmonies in raucous beauty, and teetering
in the sopranos' trills a love that shivers
and aches like a hand in a bucket of ice water.

In the kitchen window of the farmhouse
store-bought daffodils raise their yellow cornets
for the muddy tonalities of spring's chorale.

By the side of the barn are calves of old snow.
The cattle understand this melody and how
to flesh it out, this music the grass assembles.

FRAGMENTS OF LATE SPRING

Trees suspend their disbelief and hand over
excoriating leaves, each curled like a canoe,
ribbed and veined to jump lightly on the breeze,

the lines through an open palm, a leaf crinkled
like canvas over cedar, the cognitive residue
of a woodsy dispersal darkened into its own

shadow yet bright, a sunny song and dance
chorus all legs and fleshy upper arms jouncing,
notions of flippant happiness and carousing

celebration after the last exam, the leaves puppets
attached by twiggy strings like fibrous nerves,
twigs bouncing to a scherzo just to keep time.

Rabbit tracks in snow's translucence
are blue like a bruise on the limpid crust.
In the frost of afternoon's dusk
the surface crackles with snatches
of sunlight. It is early spring.
Everywhere is seasoned with pine nuts,
the buds the broken promises of winter
given to the ease of spring's munificence.
What do you know? An addiction
to the ice crystals and the way they freeze
and melt and freeze and melt and freeze.
Soon things are pulled out of a hat.

After the heavy rainfall the chuckle of the stream
is gregarious. The quilting party is in full steam
with the chatter of the sparrows and the robins
snatching up the hors d'oeuvres. The bobbins

on this old Singer unravel their threads with gaiety
in to the patchwork of the leaves. The spontaneity
a single piper plays as it stitches grass to gravel
along the bank displays water's raucous travel

as a stillness seen and seen again in a quilted stipple.
A breeze flips the patches of the fabric in a ripple
that settles into an afternoon's amiable blush.
A goldfinch conceals its yellow in a rustle of the brush.

The irises are friendly with their tongues lolling like
overheated dogs', the purple splotches paw prints
across the green linoleum, and their crania nodding
in a humid breeze so much like human heads
dipping over the languid thoughts of summer books
whose plots are crisp and narrow as the stem of an
iris might be, or a common lily, a small gesture of
yellow in the shadow of the lilac.

This is where they lift on glistening green stalks until
they star-burst into liquid gold, if gold could be
beaten into leaf so fine.

Something so light and cupped to spring to a puff
of air unnoticed but for its ruffle through the febrile
hair of a forearm. Something so much like a breath
of light that one might imagine for a moment the
metempsychosis of these little souls into two or three
butterflies.

ORANGES

The Moroccan orange wears its skin baggy,
distilled from the succulent dust
and smudged ochre of an African day.

This doubled reticence is endearing,
smaller fruit within the stunted smallness
hovering under the suspended branch.

Somehow the way it shrinks in its leather,
bashful to the touch of thumb and finger,
is more sensual than its skin-tight cousins.

The perceptible flash of colour, bright
as a startled bird, stutter of heartbeat,
condenses flavour into liquid sugar.

APPLES

The pulp of apple differs from chiseled
granite by its glistening. In the thicket
their unassuming browns and greens

bend down the grieving branches,
crooked like bones broken and never
properly set. The windfalls are strewn

across the ground like the fallen angels,
perfections that paradise couldn't hold.
The ones still hanging from the trees

are in a freeze of falling. A firmament
is deduced by one plucked and polished
on your sleeve. In its glint the curvature

of umbered sky and clouds that stretch
into glowing nebulae. You sense its
gravity by weighing it in your hand.

DANCELAND

It won't work if you do it that way,
squeezing the rough can-opener
onto the metallic sky,
hoping to spill its mackerel.

The farmers clambered up the vault
with their hoes and tilled
the rows of their potato crop,
raking the duff of weeds.

Upside down you tack
across the pearling fabric of the waves,
lose track of the wind
and find the rippling luff.

Your shirt has a rippling sleeve
and the invisible hand in a white cuff,
a pair of cufflinks,
two luminous gulls.

The open mouth and the body's huff
through a sashay of
ruffled cloud
and the tug of earth.

LADY'S-SLIPPER

A dollop of margarine scooped from a plastic tub,
the yellow too garish to be good for you. The stem
a piece of wire wrapped in green ties, bent at the neck.
But how to construct the glow that pools beneath
the long grass, the way a night light shimmers under
the mirror that reflects the sallow scar of your face?
Perhaps porcelain could be fired to just that livid yellow
that hovers above the sandy ground beside the railway
tracks. The flower is not livid, though, in its
contemplative dangle toward the skittering life
of the insect glued to the blossom's insole where
the juices are sucked right out of it. As if the billow
of the sky were a blossom pouch and the fuzz
of the prairie grass the sticky filaments; as if we
were glued to this belly, this gummy confabulation
of feral stuff, its density in the wood and its luminescence
at the edges of the leaves, this powdery fluff of confectioner
sugar. What does the fly know? In its dollop of pleasure
and terror that is the buzz of the body straining
against the world's teguments, does it need to know
the flower's forgiveness? In its hour of relapse,
does it hum a graceless tune, the hymn of its belief?
I look and look at a little yellow shoe and the print
it makes in the impressionable gravel of the mind.
Its dipper is made of the matter of star fields.
It is a globule of the sun itself, spun of the tendrils
of solar flares. Growing along the embankments,

it is a rare thing. It clings to your eyeball and keeps
you glued to its articulate totality, to its ember
of nothingness, to its return, its return, its return.

The oak tree is small; its leaves turned open
like palms, as if in a moment it shrugged
its shoulders a hundred times, perhaps to say

that the little joke of the wind's natter
is of inconsequence. We think it shouldn't
matter that the rough blister of the planet's

spin is like a top upon a table listing
in its concentric wobble. The table is made
of oak, and worn and smooth with the brush

of many palms that seek to know the treason
of the wood, the secrets it couldn't keep.
The creases on the inside of a hand branch

in the shape of a tree, so much is known.
But what hand wrought this landscaping,
this brush of lawn that sweeps across the hill

in its weightless sunlight and says, "Shadow me.
Lay your small palm of night on my shoulder."
The contusions of the weather are like

a stranger from away who settles into a house
with creaking floorboards. We didn't deserve
the hilarity of sunlight, its banter in the leaves.

FREDERICTON, OCTOBER

You are on a boardwalk on a bridge
that crosses the river. The planks creak
when you take a step and they creak

when the wind blows down river,
your pant-legs rippling the way the water does.
You are alone and then you are not alone:

there is the eccentric skirl of the wheels
of a stroller closing ground behind you,
and ahead a man who looks like chewed up

gristle, hand attached to the limp leash
of a Lab, black as a figment of woods.
There is a bicycle and a bobbing of knees,

the glide of the helmet that glints of metallic
blue. And then the thud of a jogger,
his breath a chuff of wool woven into his

small hat. The family mutt strains
for the little girl's cracker, but the girl
stares at her mother, whose arms are folded

over a grey sweatshirt that reads *Fredericton
High School Band.* You hear all the talk
that hovers over the town like evening mist.

A gull is hugging the air and you turn again,
and there she is, your wife, like a line
from a half-remembered country tune.

Now is a time of thinness, the treetops
barely diagramming the parts of speech.

This the substratum of the way we speak
the keener edges of longer nights,

of vivid greens blanched to paler
orange and yellows. The remnants

of a cow in a stockyard drained of blood.
Maple leaves holding to heat's memory,

the way the day was fat with sunlight,
gone like a cloud of summer gnats.

A shriveled pear has leaked its juice
upon a paving stone and the buzz

of a late wasp is below the threshold
of hearing, the wings slower as if its

battery were wearing down. Autumn
rains have settled into a smother of

low-lying thoughtfulness unmoving
in the sky, the street a matte of charcoal.

When the fire engine scuttled past,
it seemed it could not control the blaze,

the siren screamed of the urgent trees
bursting everywhere with saintliness.

A GLASS OF WATER

When you say you need water you are speaking
of the ordinary, not the fine spray of a nozzle
wisping the delicate petals in the garden,

nor the faint drizzle that is not quite fog, not quite rain.
You are likely thinking of a glass, of a liquid
sliding over that itch in your throat.

But then you notice the glass itself is water.
Its waves rippling, you can see the flow of it,
its little turbulences, its shallow remembrance

of silicon dioxide. It is, as the physicists would say,
"a supercooled liquid, rather than a true solid."
If you drop it, it sounds like an ocean against the rocks.

There is too much water, we think. We need
to take it away in drains, sewers, sluices and pipes.
But sometimes there is a thirst like a pair of scissors

cutting across the fabric of the throat. Then water
seeps into a sheet of paper and infiltrates its fibres,
gently tugging them apart and language

dissolves. It soaks the very air we breathe,
humidity as thick as a wool suit on a summer's
day. A glass of cold water has the capability

to condense droplets right out of the air.
It is so innocuous sitting there on the table.
It belongs to everyone, its sweat on a thick day

seems a sweat without work, an imaginary ease.
So many have never seen a glass of water,
they have so little of it. Will we ever hold

it in our hands again in this form of amnesia?
You forget its dribble into the future. It is the pure
source of the present, its transparent anguish.

THE CONVECTION OF THE SOUL

*The Okavango River flows from Angola to the swamplands of
Botswana, where it dries up without reaching the sea.*

There is a place so dry that a tropical flood
of water will choke on its own sediment,
thickening in a delicatessen of mud.

A river sometimes disappears into a fumble
of heat. It forgets itself, but you cannot
forget that labouring music, an organ

pumping its reedy breath. And in the low flats
where the water pauses in its growing thirst
you see the grasses, a glossary of weeds

brushed by a mere notation of the wind.
They stand like an octave of obsolete ideas,
but how greenly given in a land of straw.

In a sky like this a cloud is an awkward
reminiscence of a fresh thoughtless rain
plump in a crinoline of purple moisture.

III

SLEEPING OVER

I was still in sleep's pillowed conservatory
when I heard the plunk of a few keys
on the old piano my father used to play.

The ice on the slender branches of the trees
outside my window made an awkward clack
much like his fingers yellowed in disease

clicking a scrawny tune that he recalled from back
before the war. I know that music, I thought,
and I rose, recalling how we used to yak

about his complicated past, a convoluted plot
of the Depression and a war, the day trips he
and my mum took to ski, where they caught

the fall of gravity's plumb line. Never so free,
they thought, as they shaved snow in clean arcs
carved over moguls. It had meant little to me

then. I found him by the piano, soft sparks
glimmering in his eyes, that cock-eyed grin
as if he were about to tell a joke, marks

on his face I didn't recognize. Ugly as sin,
he said, and curled his fingers to play
"What a beautiful morning," his voice so thin.

Yesterday I stood by the marsh
to take my measure
and I felt afraid,
even as the wind placed its hand
on my head and whispered,
"there, there."

And there it was, the marsh
quivering with red-winged blackbirds
in the cruise of their feathers,
latching onto the springboard of the rushes,
a pair of northern pintails
vanishing into a quiet swallow
of water and popping up
into their buoyancy.

I had never seen so many birds
and kinds of birds, as if
a hundred children played
on penny whistles.

Back at the cottage a sparrow
rips at the exposed and matted
cotton of an old tarp
covering the gas barbeque.

It seems the metaphor of smallness,
but a sparrow is not so small
as it is common, plain-looking,
browns and greys like a ball
of dust gathered under the bed.
It is bigger than that flash
of sunlight we call goldfinch.

So if it is small, it is a great smallness,
a creaturely smallness,
a smallness made to snuggle
into a nest it makes for itself.

I wish that I could find
that ease, that flicker and lift,
the flit from branch to twig,
a smudge of intelligence
in the canopy.

RACCOON

This particular stretch of land is uninhabited.
Spruce trees are a cross-cut set of teeth that tear
across the horizon, a violence in the backwoods

understood all too well. The raccoon paddles
by the side of the road, absorbed in its own ideas,
a professor pawing the pages of an old book.

It is late, and in front of the car a pool of light
softens the creature's luminescent rings
as if some purpose posed its binaries in the bristle

of this clever and inquisitive scavenger probing
the bank of the highway. All full of questions
and the answers it finds are scraps of carrion.

It snuffles the night and in a quarrel of darkness
you couldn't agree more, to rub your hand over
the fur hanging in the hall closet, to ruffle the words

and comb them back, to sound them, to ring
the buzzer of your friends' house and discover
no one's home, and it's all right, it's Saturday

and they're at the bar. You drive this length
of road through the brush of trees, puzzled
to happen on this incarnate of night's imperium.

JANUARY SONG

I know something of melancholy, its dendritic
half-truths, its musky odour

of week-old bread. It has two faces
that are too close, like two lovers

who kiss past the expiration of desire,
are still kissing now, lips slightly chapped.

The past and the future have collapsed,
like the leafy mulch of a world war.

It comes like an airborne division
opening its parachutes over the open fields.

It takes possession of our telecommunications
days after the gaiety of our tea and crumpets.

I decide to sip at the edges of a camomile tea,
because sadness is like an extra hour of sleep

in the morning. I wish I could belong to a great
age of melancholy, to let my aching puddles of fat

sink onto the fainting couch and think "Genius!"
Like a god it exists everywhere and nowhere.

THAT DIRT ROAD

I would prefer not to go down
    that dirt road without my
little red wagon. My battered tin
    lunch pail says I have somewhere
to go, but I don't want to go down
    that dirt road without my
protractor set, you know, and my
    compass. I'm going down, and crying
can't make me stay in this
    alfalfa, I'm going down that
dirt road. I would prefer not.
    To go down that dirt road without
my pink chewable eraser and its
    sumptuous rubbery soya curd
dryness would be so naked and you know
    I would prefer not to go down
that dirt road without my Huckleberry
    Hound T-shirt. The buttercups
that grow by the ditch don't go down
    that dirt road. They hold fast
where they're soiled. The forsythia
    by the corner of the veranda doesn't
go down. It rockets up in a golden sting
    of flowers careening into holiday
fireworks. The forget-me-nots and heal-all
    don't go down that dirt road.
I would prefer not to go down that dirt road.

Tell me, Mr Sol, where you were last night.
I woke up this morning
and your clothes weren't fitting you right.
The west wind curled the leaves of corn.
The field mice scuttled through the stalks.
The malignant cows coughed in the barn.
The dog clicked across the linoleum floor.
The moths spun cotton around the yellow light.
The crickets scratched their hind-leg ache.
The maples stretched their limbs in a hush.
The sky bristled its hair like a cat.
The moon crusted the house in its chemical white.

The brutality of jazz is concealed
in the saxophone's breezy sunlight,
the clarinet's reedy shadow by the lake.
It is like money laundering, the way
the music saunters from the back alley
into the high-school sock hop.
That the body's sheen can reek
and be so clean. It's the froth
of a soap commercial, its artifice
of bubbles arranged around the tops
of the breasts, arms waving like the branches
of palm trees. The nostalgia of jazz,
the rush of heroin, it's the spike of fun,
the invention of patio furniture.
Don't you just love it, black shoes
and a white dress shirt and the spin
and shimmy. Let's go for a drive
in the cool night air. I can see in your eyes
that you're feeling a little blue.
The click of the cigarette case, the scratch
of a light, it flickers across the dark
of your face. It's all too much, isn't it?

Even the word skyscraper is a nostalgia for the urban.
The reflective glass of the towers domesticates
space by giving back the cozy blues and browns
of an afternoon walking the disorienting streets.
Downtown is so ethereal it's no longer massive—
has become a suburb of itself. You feel at home,
find a store for all thirty-one teams of the NFL.
The cherry red of the street cars rumbles past
the display windows and the mannequins posed
in a squeal of delight. It's a festival of chocolate!
If you want a taste of the earth itself, eat a truffle.
The cliché of signage is marvellous, delightful
in its happy applause. Everything for a dollar?
Remember when plastic used to be pejorative?
We like plastic now, or at least I do, for its deeply
luminiferous qualities, and for the pliable way
it embodies the concept of flex time. You can buy
a hundred and forty-seven plastic containers
for twenty-nine ninety-nine. The windows
of the towers are mirrored in silver or copper,
and dangling in the middle air are two specks
of humanity washing windows. On the sidewalk
by the ramshackle store the shopkeeper is washing
his window. On the street a splash of kids are
washing car windows with their squeegees.
Fruit spills onto the sidewalk in wooden crates—
the expected oranges and grapefruits, but also guava

and plantain, and three or four misplaced coconuts.
No one can plan the feeding of a city: it has to happen
spontaneously, in a ruckus of container ports and
delivery trucks. Some fall through the cracks.
But this is what we pass by all the time—the smell
of the alley and the feeble air through the sidewalk
grates, the decomposing slick of discarded food.
Afternoon light sparkles through the warm layers
of particulate and sprawls lavishly on the pavement
dust. The picture of the city is edged in jagged
abutments, the glisten of plate glass, the squaring
of corners wherever the eye looks, the joy of repeating
right angles that frame and give luster and depth
to the painting the eye makes of it all, that makes it
look so fresh, so fresh and clean. And they do seem
to scrape the sky, the towers bronzed in late light,
the sky itself a diorama of tissue paper and cotton
batting, as if fleetingly suspended in a window display.
The mood is exquisitely inflationary, just like the rent.

THE MAN WORE A HAT. THE WOMAN DIDN'T.

The cat rippled through the raspberry canes.
Here I am at home, it thought. The various
patches of grass and flower talked jaunty stories
about their underground affairs and a winter
that stayed all season long. What a banana.
Sex, is that all you think about! Limp petunias.
Squirrels flounce about the dropped pears,
listening to a sighing juice seep into the earth.
Cats, I notice, don't creep up on squirrels.
They amble in foreknowledge, arriving where
the squirrel is going to go. Rousseau, Rousseau.
A bee cruises the pathetically flimsy blossoms.
He's not from around here. Not a thought
for tomorrow, everything is bleeding green.

                    I held a knife
over the sink where it dripped
a pale water and the syrup of a seed
stuck to the stainless blade, a seed,
a plenipotentiary of the improbable
balance, the knife cantilevered
in my hand, and there was the
flesh of my waking dream
in a melon.
                    If the fruit were a bowl
full of rubies and sapphires and the blood
of a single garnet, a sampling of pearls
in creamy iridescence, would you say
no, turn your bitter lips, would you close
your eyes and drift into the oblivious
welter of your thoughts?
                              Nor could I.
I spoke a glossolalia of the rind and pulp,
the pale scent of a watercolour orange,
the faint sugar of the juice that fills
and drains from the back of your mouth.
In the glint of the blade I found belief
in a melon's sorrow and as it echoed
from the countertops and kitchen walls
I listened to the cacophony of yellow-
purple birds edged in emerald sheen.

The branches of the oak fire to a glowing yellow
in the February sun. It is late afternoon.

You don't think thoughts; they think themselves
in the infinitesimal calculus of the synapses.

I sang myself to sleep the night my father died.
I invented him and continue to invent him now.

It was day after day of crisp sun, followed by the sobbing
violence of rain. I had no thoughts at that moment.

They can find your thoughts with an electroencephalogram.
Think harder! Think: the branches of an oak.

Chocolate dribbles across the shallow cake
where the oils harden from a molten glisten
to a dull matte, warmer currents in a lake
of sugar icing buttered yellow. You listen
to a wind buff and ripple curling waves.
Lucid, frothy, cool and fabulously dense,
the surface layers fathoms over liquid graves
of flecked chocolate buried in the sediments
of spongy white. The candles bob and wink
each their own unique complaint, the danger
of the shoals, the unexpected years. You blink
and your oldest friend becomes a stranger.
Dark chocolate cuts the sweet with a little bitter.
It doesn't matter. You celebrate the moment's glitter.

AFTER THE DANCE

The pavillion vanished, but the outer stairs
remain. They ascend briefly into air and stop
as if restrained by their own railing, apparition

of some forgotten thought, some notion
that seemed a promise of delight and lofty
fun, now hung with planters and a few

petunias dangling from the worn bannister,
suggesting that even dumb ideas are splashed
with colour and carry some relation to a garden.

The flowers are tenderly fluffed and mended
by diligent workers who arrive with hoses
and watering cans, whistling a refrain popular

in their youth, a tune they might have danced to
in crisp suits, newly cut carnations fastened
to the lapels, before emigration and children.

One wouldn't think that one patch of sand
could hide so many. Bent over like bobbing
toys, the diggers work the square yard

in front of them, scrabbling after the clams
that squirt deeper into the alluvial muck,
the way a god might grapple to save souls,

flinging them aside into a plastic bucket
with a careless shrug of the shoulders.
This is the definition of seasonal work.

Sun bakes the flats as the tide recedes;
it sears the skin at the back of the neck,
bronzes the hair along the muscles

of the arm. I mimicked this employment
as a boy, shiny red plastic shovel and a big
yellow pail dangling from my puffy hand.

But I couldn't help lifting my eyes to this
nothing, nothing, nothing that swills across
a blank expanse. The furious diggers seem bent

on repeated calculations of pi in each glance
at a clam's circumference. Their tiny plots
anticipate an inheritance in this life

and the next. Not much in this life, which
pays them piecemeal. As gravity drags
its linen over the clam beds, the yammering

pistons of an ATV race across the sand to gather
the day's catch. I wonder—they must stiffen—
does their world close in on them like a glassy shell?

At low tide, the water's sibilance is a distant memory,
last year's jays at the feeder. Along the back road
paint peels from the clapboard. The man on his porch,

his house shriveling behind him, wood the colour
of ash flicked from a cigarette, had ribs like this,
the sand hard, damp, exposed like a washboard.

And it is a washboard, a few wisps of seaweed
pasted to the corrugated piece of tin, snagged
thread from a blouse or shag from a mop sagging

into the bucket's soup, and look closely, leftover suds
bubbled across the sand. The ridges dig into the arches
of your feet—it's like standing on the rungs of a ladder.

This is not compassion, this scrabble of glitter, it is
grief's seepage, the abusive beauty of the backwater
made over for a tourist's careless transience.

Then gradually the sea comes nearer, momentary
affluence covering the old poverty, an opportunistic
welter of life cruising the tide's surge to the newly

revealed feeding grounds, the seeming back-broken
life submerged in both its anger and love, the tide's
engine grinding its gears along the road's gravel.

THE PALE GREEN ROWBOAT

There is a creak in the bed
as you shift in the drowsy light
of the lamp
by which you were reading,
the book curled by your chin, the pages papery thin.

A slim breeze worries and teases
the loose threads
of a nightgown, whispers
uncertainties in the leaves of the pear,
wears its fearful measure into the evening hour.

Ours is a tethered love
in a length of rope that ties the boat
to shore. You tug on the rope
of your dream and feel its sinew
and grit and you almost hear the creak
of the boat and the lapping water. Do I step gently

enough when I remove
the oars from the oarlocks of your sleeping
muscles, when I click off the light, when I place the book
in the shelf's dark corner?
And when the rumble of your
breathing stops for a moment,
do I speak lightly enough to hold that catch in your throat?

A WEDDING POEM

for Jeffery & Annette

It's the way you imagined it to be: a road
runs into the forest, into summer's lazy
complications of brush along the ditches.

The road is gravel and dust has stained
the bracts and sepals of the flowering weeds.
A dusty sunlight has settled onto the spruce.

As you walk you cannot see into the spruce;
their branches interlock and they're closely
packed, but you arrive into the openness

of a crossroads—not a fork and the difficult
choices—but a place where other more casual
lives are imaginable, a place where two roads

intersect, which implies habitation to the right
and left, villages you don't intend to visit,
but are pleased to envision their endurance.

And being at a crossroads, there is a store
and provisions, tins of soup, an axe, some matches,
which the grocer places in musty paper bags.

Outside there are a couple of houses with yards,
and a dog barking. You carry on your way,
and as you round a bend in the road you pause

to look forward and back, and there is the road
as straight and as true as you can see into it,
stretching to a point you always knew was there.

The twist of the cord lends strength
to the stem, which binds itself in a weave
of intimacy and reaches along its length
toward a core of seed. We want to believe

that a pear doesn't drop to prove gravity;
in undulation it bellies out and hangs
by a thread; it leans against the depravity
of autumn's ultimate proof. The pangs

of an unearthed desire shimmer in the gloss
of their fainting green skin. They wish to lift
themselves to the sky, they want to cross
over, to sparkle along an orchard's drift.

When they do fall, they slip from a glove
of air, giving their broken fibres to love.

I V

The Horizons of Tragedy

"… for pity is aroused by unmerited misfortune,
fear by the misfortune of a man like ourselves."

—ARISTOTLE, *Poetics*

Was this, then, to be our first principle,
that suffering makes human the echoing

woods? The shiver of the leaves in a summer
rain, the unison of their hushed cry,

told us to seize these articulate weapons.
Then an incomprehensible fire exploded

across the treetops, leaving the spent
matchsticks, the smouldering ash. Later,

in the new growth, willows bend to drink
from the brook. They see a distorted face.

UNITY

When the wind picked up that spring day
it plucked the pear blossoms from the tree

and scattered them across the yard. It made
a visible difference. This was the middle

of the story, after the flowers but before
the fruit. The petals caught in your hair,

shifted through the grass like an early snow.
Beginnings derive from familiar unknowns

and middles end in uncertain terrain.
For now, a pear is the organic whole.

HAMARTIA

The mind devours the vastness of the sky,
or it longs to, to see the distance of the stars

and galaxies flattened like kernels of grain
sprinkled across the shadowed floor of an old

silo. We know these stars to be the ovens
of the soul. The careless flick of a cigarette

ignites the subsequent explosion and so
the hero is spent in the waste of an idea.

A flame cupped in the hand, the spark of fireflies
ascending from the mistake of the weeds.

PLOT

The invitation was printed in gold embossed
letters, indicating casual attire to be acceptable.

You wonder if you are early or late,
and if either might be advantageous,

like certain species of flower that uncoil
in spring mud or linger after the first frost

to avoid midsummer's rush hour. And what
of flowers that overrun their boundaries,

spilling into the thicket of purple irises?
You are not a guest, you find, after the fact.

CHARACTER

The profile of the face was stamped in bronze
as if on a coin. When the light in November

has such a lustre, you know you are
better than yourself. It is in the clarity

of the fish pond after the leaves have fallen,
the warmth of the sun on your deserving skin.

The coin was tossed in spring, and so you are
not watching its casual loopings through heads

and tails, nor will you watch when it is found
impacted in the water's new sheet of ice.

THOUGHT

The self spins out its little comedies
like twists of old newspaper tumbling

in a preposterous aeolian wind.
These are the ghosts of a moment so brief

they vanish before they are contemplated.
But there was a more serious thought,

that almost held once in the canopy
of an elm tree, that even denuded of its

leafy verbiage maintained a stark nobility,
the misunderstood branchings of its disease.

DICTION

The first word spoken is the most true.
The others spoken in the follow-through

are full of life's complications, a zoo
of quibbling parakeets, a simmering brou-

haha of chimpanzees, a brackish slough
of amphibian and reptilian creatures who

lurk in the rustling grass. A sky this blue
should resolve itself into a simple hue.

A scribbling cirrus of cloud wriggles a few
lines in a stormy scrawl. It's nothing new.

MELOPEIA

The squeal of the peepers in a spring night
is minimalist music. It is the honing

of a blade that is never quite sharp enough.
It must be ground again so it can slice

through flesh with at least a partial forgiveness.
The shrill of the tea kettle is too loud,

or too singular to be this noise, but the sound
of endless boiling contains the throb of it.

The reeds vibrate with that strange melody,
that sounds as if it were made by the mud itself.

SPECTACLE

The breezes that bustle about the trees
are the costumers, of course; they turn and fold

the leaves or give a quick tug at a lapel,
last-minute adjustments to a sleeve too short

to carry the gesture of the day, the weeds
that kick their greenery in time to the air's baton.

How trivial, and yet if we could only imitate
the flounce and sparkle of such a performance,

what happiness. We give the arrangement
our quiet applause as the lights go down.

PERIPETEIA

All too often a cloud cover is incomplete,
leaks light at the edges, afterglow of some

conflagration of which only the birds could
have knowledge. You see them in the twilight

pecking at the plowed rows of field hardening
in frost, a dust of snow, unexpectedly early.

What kind of seeds could they be picking at?
A simple lack of imagination makes me ask

the question. The birds cannot stay long.
The sun glints in the windows of the houses.

ANAGNORISIS

When a river doubles back on itself,
or is ambushed by the muddy current

of another watershed, there is an anguish
in the turbulence, a casual ripping across

the surface, like ligaments pulling loose
from the bone. You didn't see it coming.

It is a miscarriage of one's expectations,
the murmur of a lengthening spring evening

after dark, thinking of the afternoon's tulip
bending to the weight of its own blossom.

CATHARSIS

You were crying by the river, watching
the swollen river shadows carry with them

the bodies of the dead. The willow leaves
whispered like a radio in the long hours

of the night. You listened for the consoling
calm. You'd always known this brutality—

it breaks open in the spectacle of a new day.
You wanted nothing more than a larger heart,

but your suffering is only that of a single
blade of grass washed by the rain's catastrophe.

Acknowledgements

Some of these poems have appeared in earlier versions in the
journals *The Antigonish Review, ARC, Grain, The Harpweaver, The
Malahat Review* and *Vallum* or in the anthologies *Landmarks, Why
I Sing the Blues, Listening with the Ear of the Heart* and *Vintage 1999.*
Two poems appeared in English and French in *Ellipse* and
I thank Marylea MacDonald for the translations.

I have lost count of how many people have helped me in
the revision of these poems. I thank all of you. I would like
to thank specifically six people who edited the manuscript
from beginning to end: Sabine Campbell, Anne Compton,
Anne Simpson, Sue Sinclair, David Solway and my editor at
Gaspereau Press, Andrew Steeves.

I would like to thank the participants of the Ice House
Workshop for your insights and encouragement. Thanks
also to "Conversation and Silence" colloquium at
St. Peter's College and the Leighton Studios at the
Banff Centre for the Arts.

The Banff Centre for the Arts, the Canada Council for the
Arts, the New Brunswick Arts Board and the University of New
Brunswick provided funding toward the writing of this book.

Typeset in Baskerville by Andrew Steeves
& printed offset at Gaspereau Press.

Gaspereau Press acknowledges the support of the
Canada Council for the Arts, the Nova Scotia Department of
Tourism & Culture and the Government of Canada through the
Book Publishing Industry Development Program.

7   6   5   4   3   2   1

Library and Archives Canada Cataloguing in Publication

Leckie, Ross, 1953–
Gravity's plumb line / Ross Leckie.
Poems.

ISBN 1-55447-002-1
I. Title.

PS8573.E3377G73 2005   C811'.54
C2005-900037-6

GASPEREAU PRESS PRINTERS & PUBLISHERS
47 CHURCH AVENUE, KENTVILLE, NOVA SCOTIA
CANADA B4N 2M7   WWW.GASPEREAU.COM